Hello!
I am a horse.

I0108785

The average lifespan of a horse is around 25 to 30 years.

But some horses have lived much longer.

Come visit us.

Horses live in many different places around the world, like farms, ranches, and even in the wild.

Horses are herbivores.

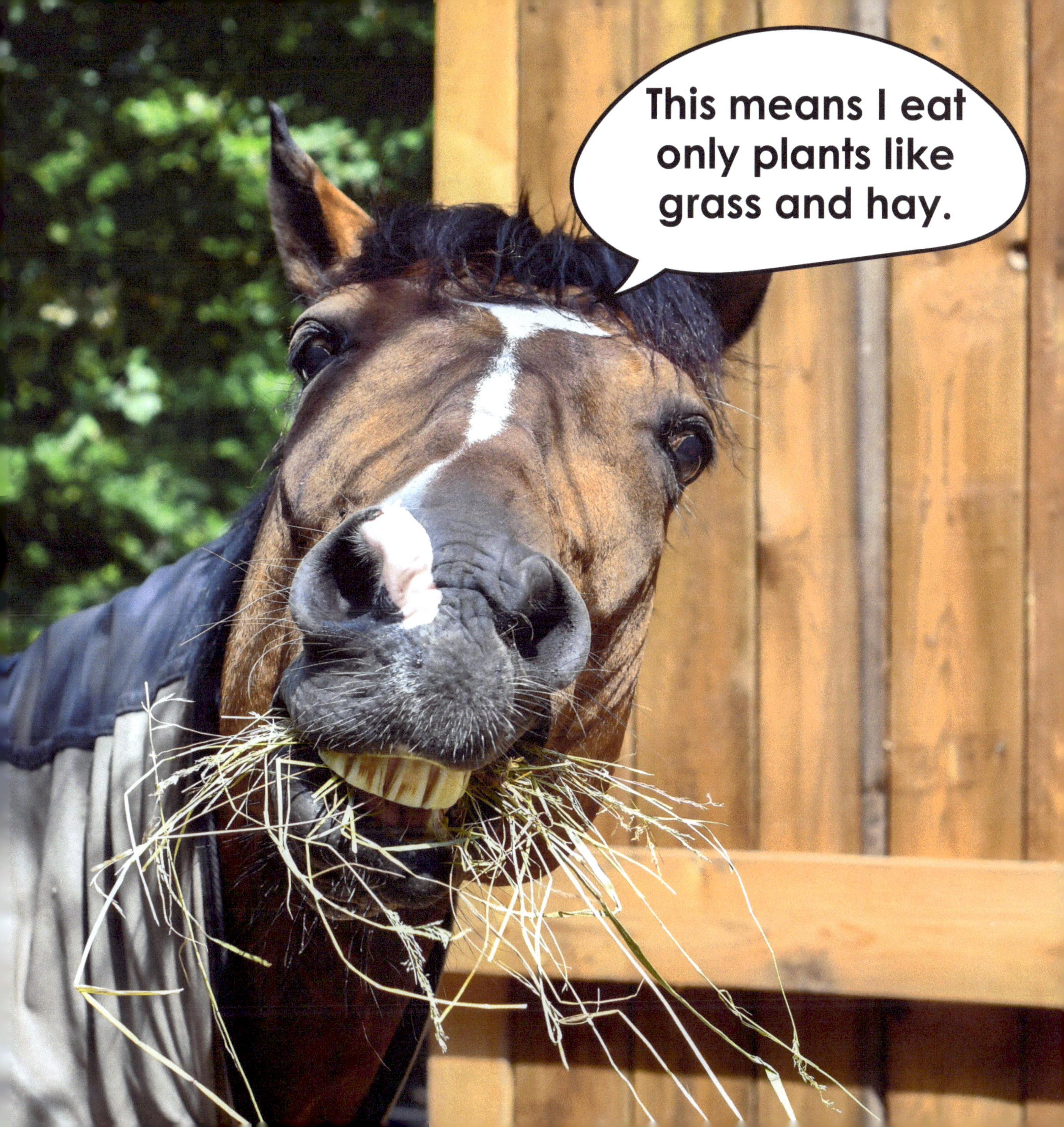
This means I eat only plants like grass and hay.

Horses have been domesticated for thousands of years.

People use horses for transportation, farming, and sport.

We have a job to do

Horses can see almost 360 degrees around them.

I have excellent eyesight.

Horses' eyes are positioned higher on their head compared to other animals.

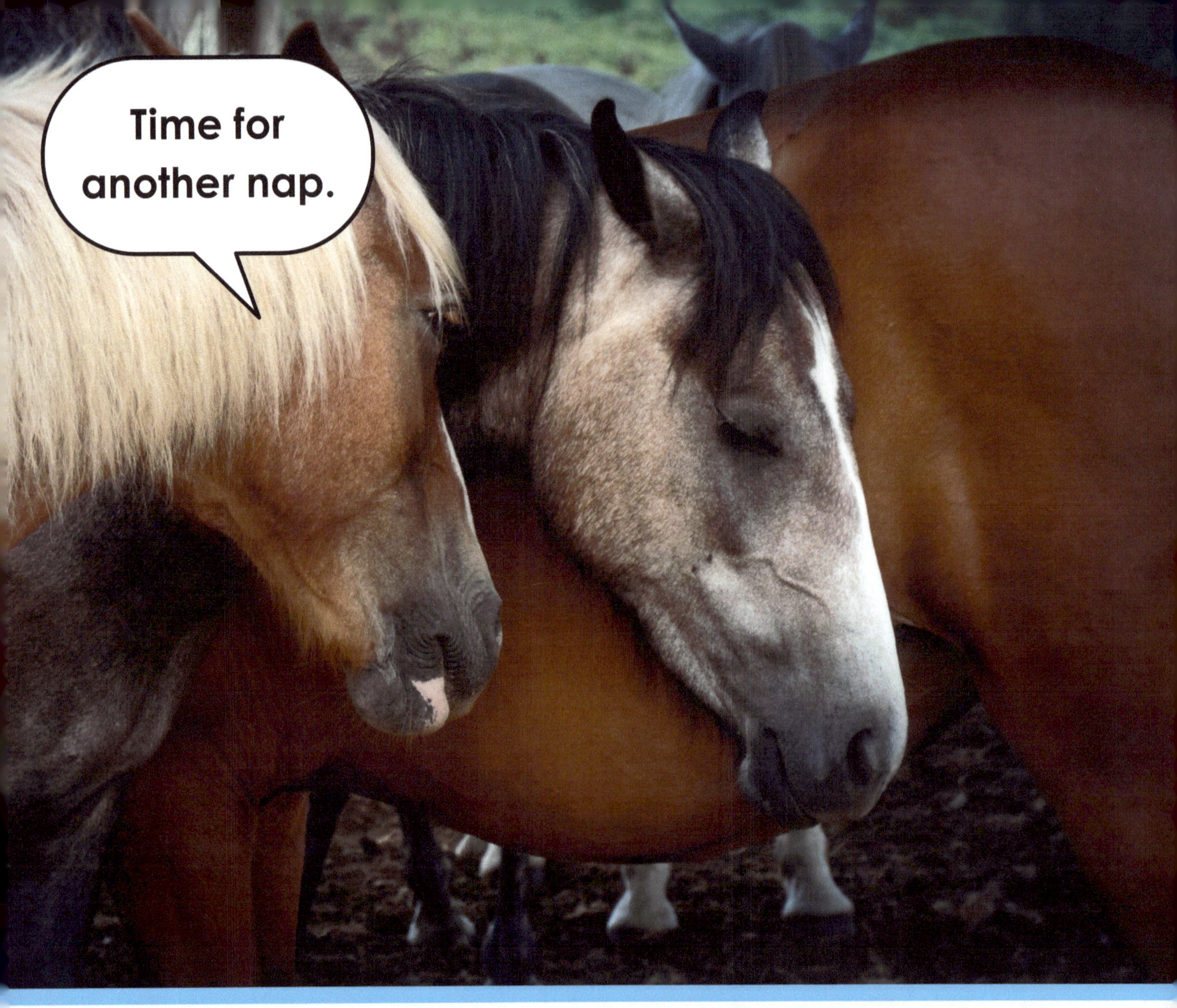
Time for another nap.

Horses can sleep standing up.

Horses have a unique way of sleeping called "catnapping". They sleep for short periods throughout the day and night.

Horses have a strong bond with their owners.

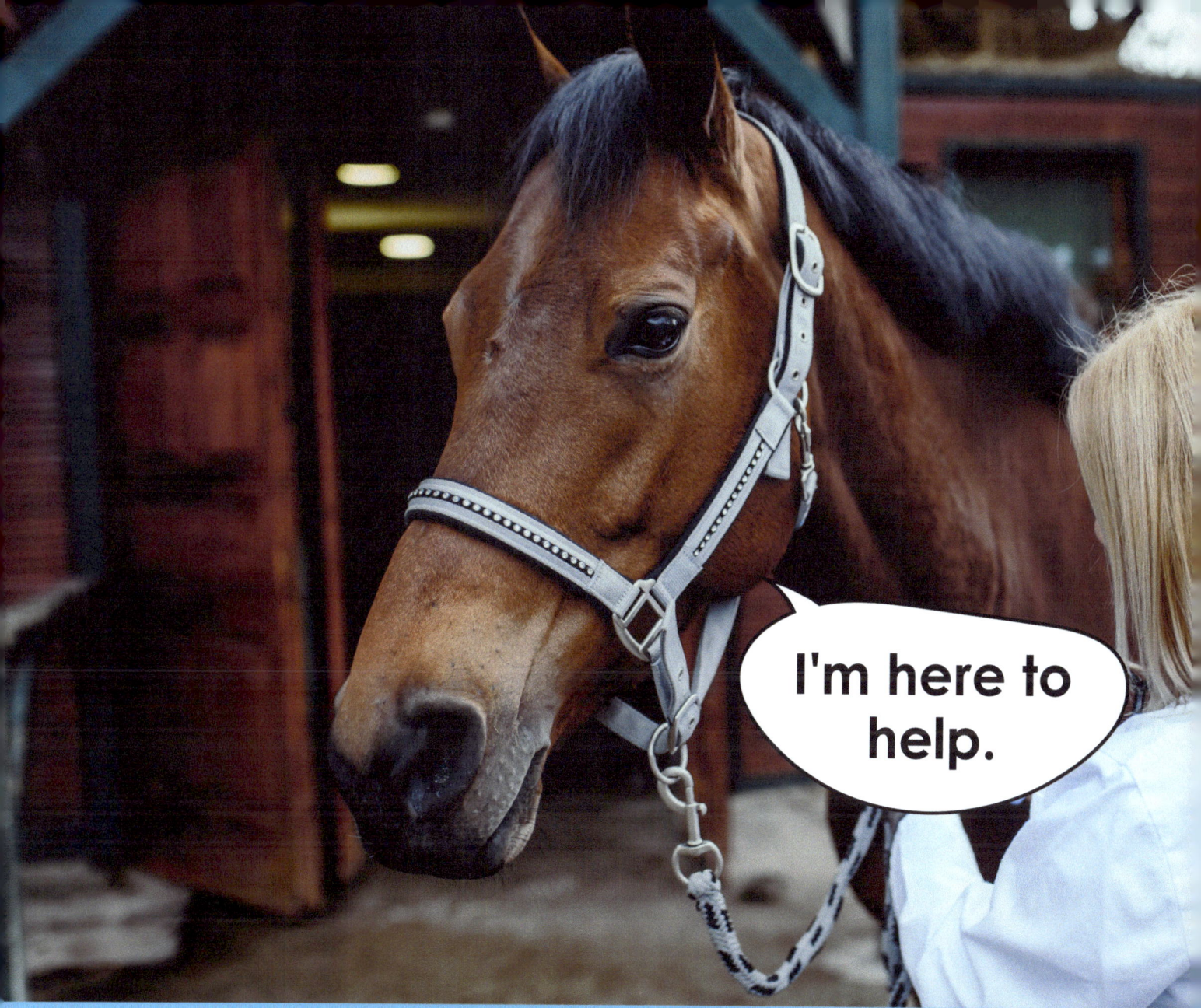

I'm here to help.

Horses have been used to help people feel better about themselves.

Horses have a strong sense of hearing.

We can hear all around us.

Horses can rotate their ears to listen in different directions.

Horses have different coat colors and patterns.

Horse fur can be solid colors, spots, and stripes.

Some horses can run up to
55 miles (89km) per hour.

We are fast runners.

Horses have a natural ability to swim.

Horses live in groups called "herds".

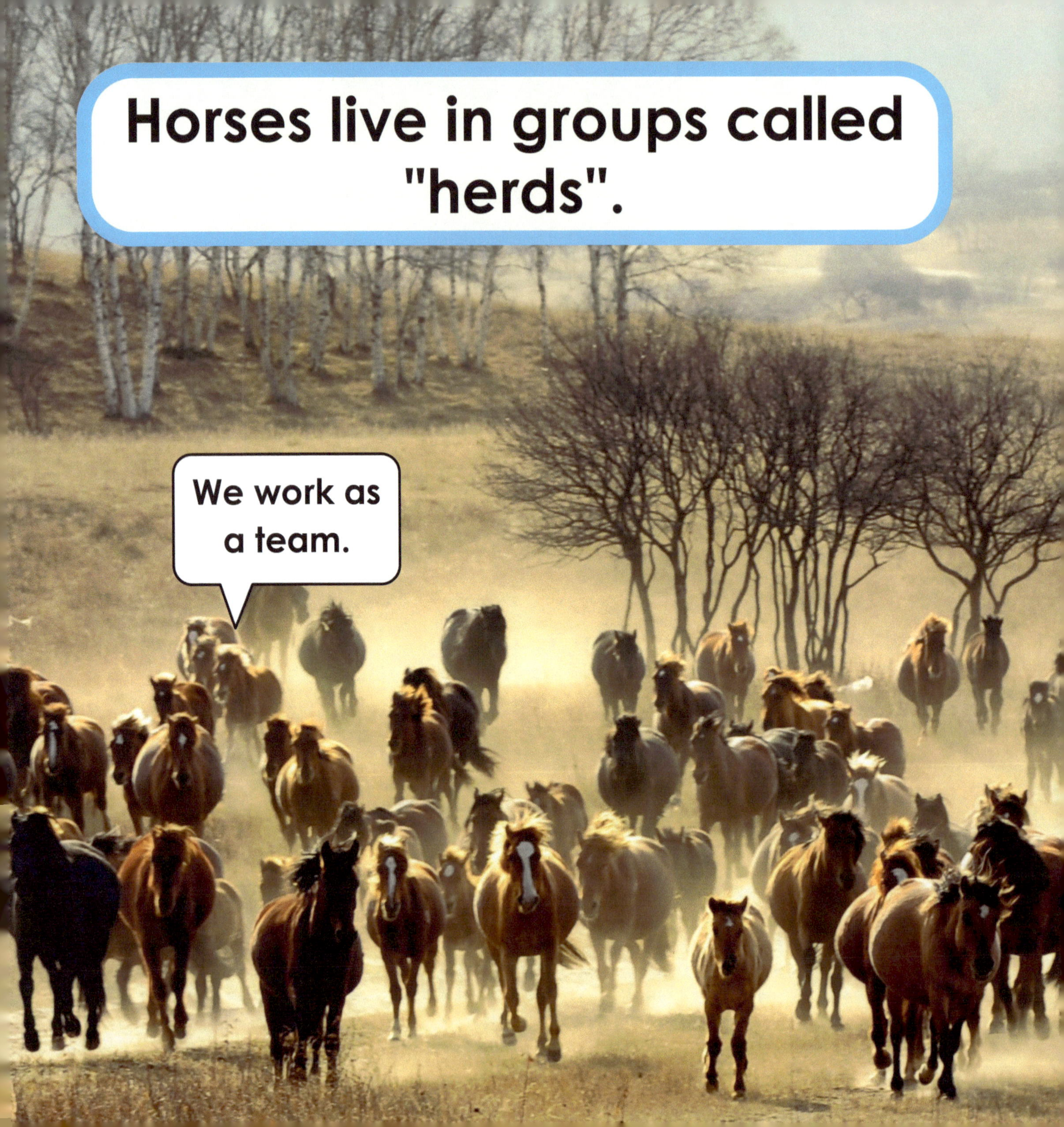

Stronger horses in the herd lead the others.

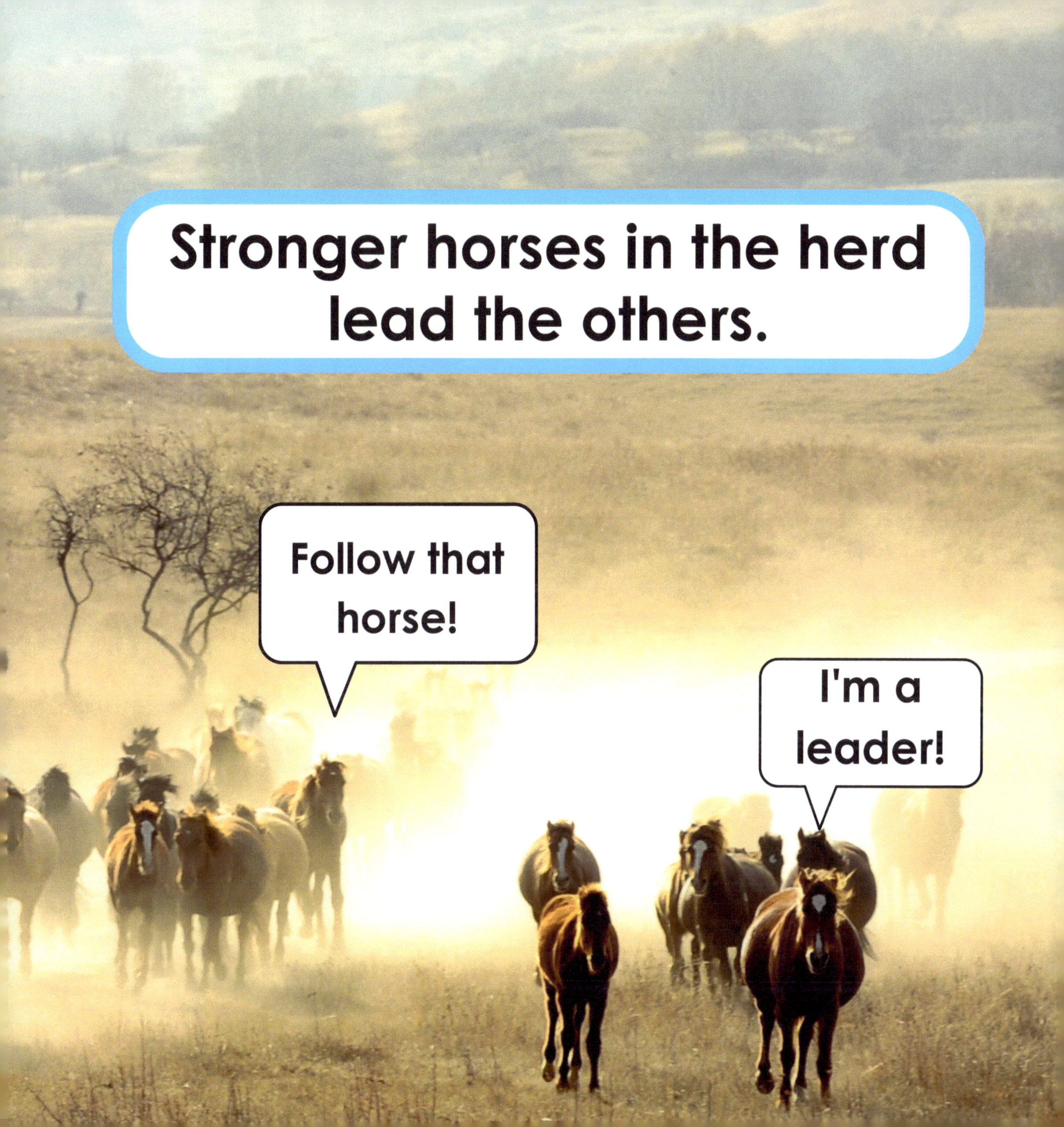

Horses like to groom each other by using their teeth and lips to scratch and clean.

I love you.

Horses show affection by nuzzling and licking.

Horses communicate with each other using body language and sounds.

A baby horse is called a "foal".

Foals can recognize their mothers by their smell and voice.

Horses can sense danger.

Horses warn the rest of the herd and lead them to safety.

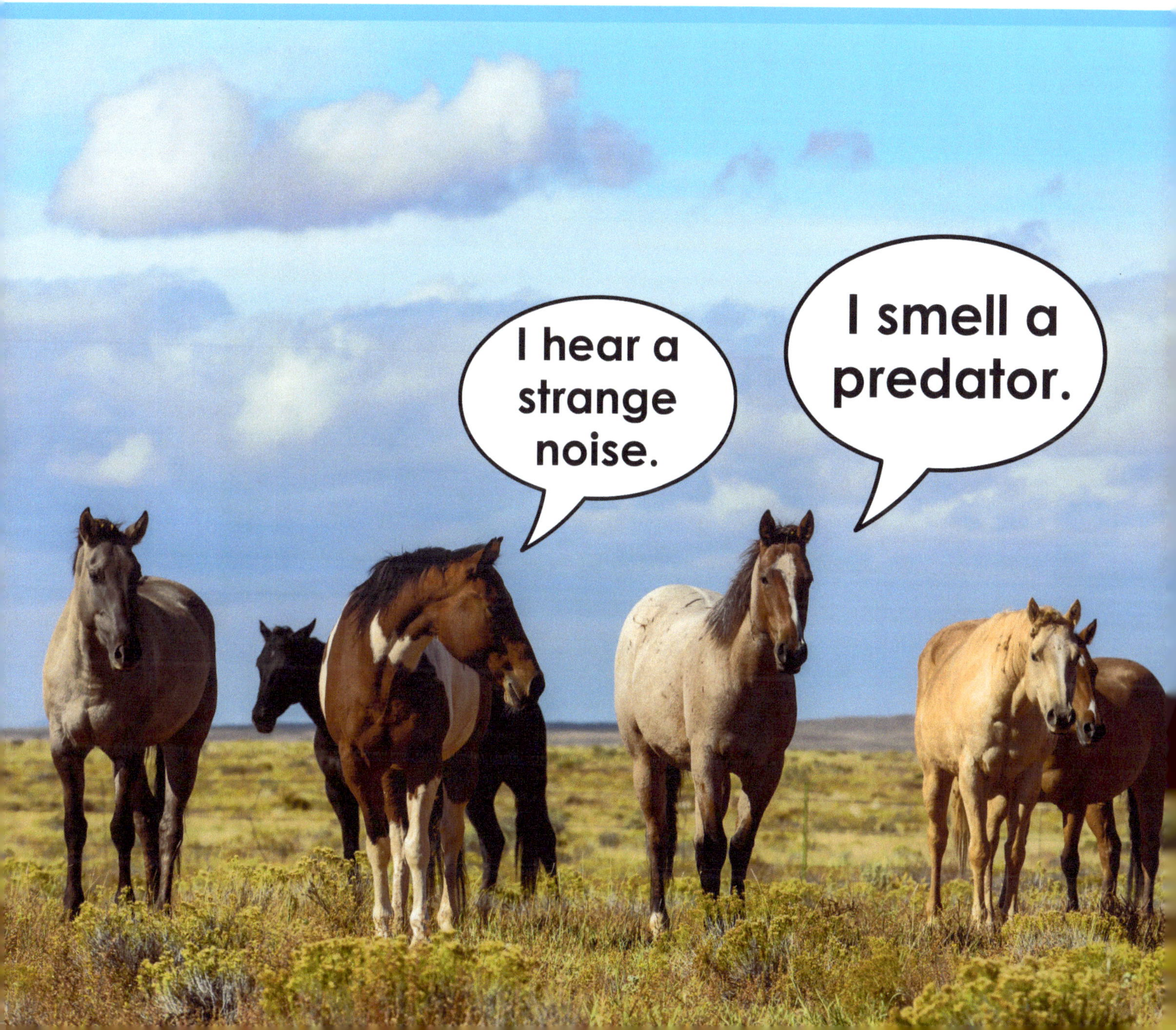

Horses have an incredible memory.

Horses can remember people and places for a very long time.

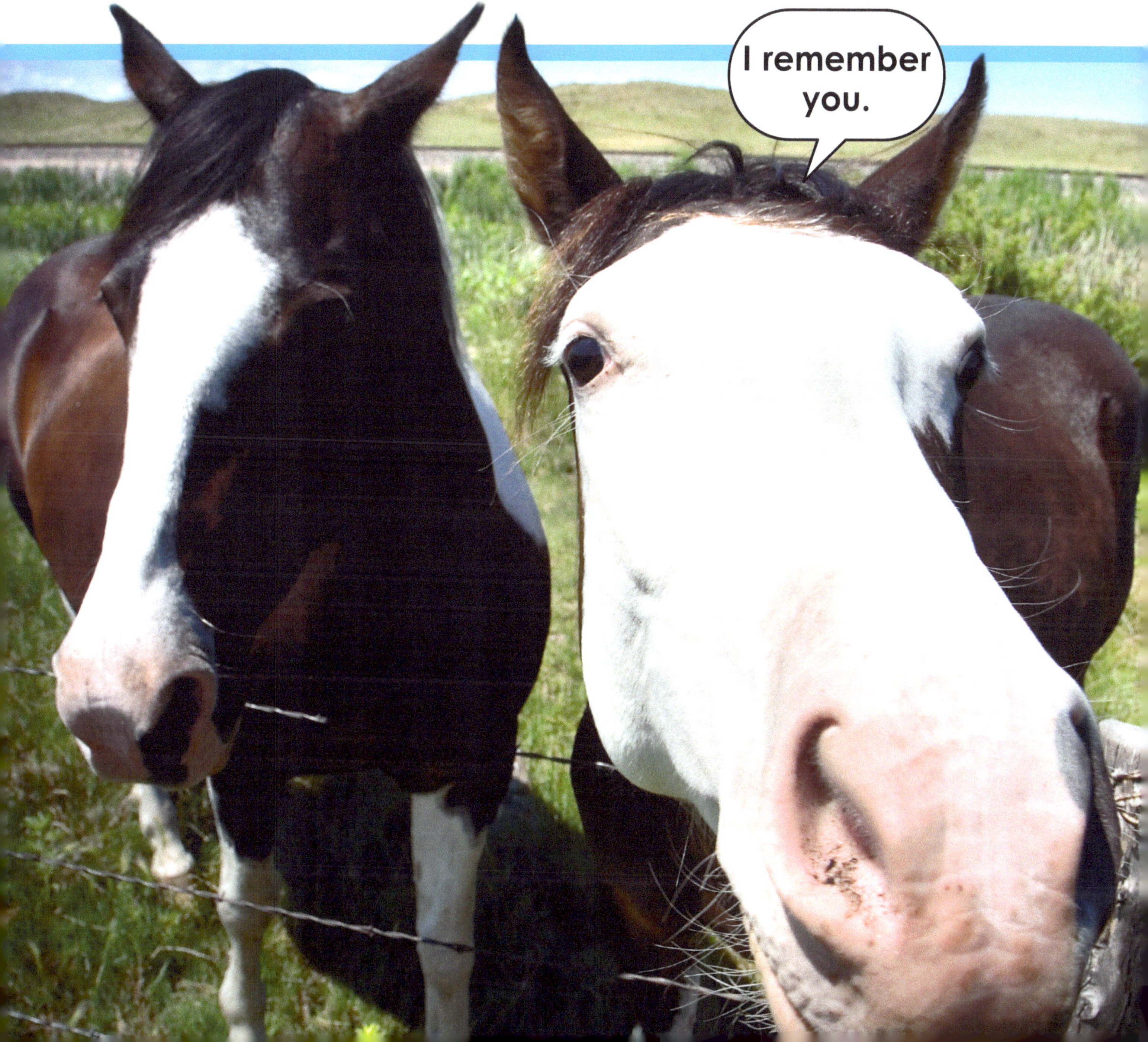

I am a horse.
Goodbye!

Want more?

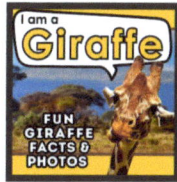      

 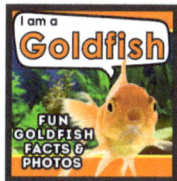     

 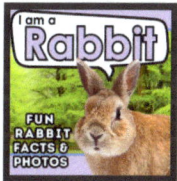    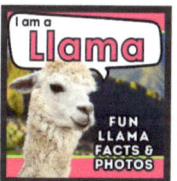 

       ... and more

COLLECT THEM ALL!
ActiveBrainsBooks.com

Hello parents!

Visit us to find out about new releases and **FREE** offers. We'll let you know when we have a new release coming out and how you can get it for FREE.

And you can cast your vote for what book we make next!

scan here

ActiveBrainsBooks.com

or visit here

---

scan here

Let us know what you think. As an independent publisher, your honest reviews mean a lot to us and our business. We'd love to hear from you!

amazon.com/review/create-review/

or visit here

FOLLOW US on Amazon.

amazon.com/author/activebrainsbooks

ActiveBrainsBooks.com

ACTIVE BRAINS